GOODBYE, UKULELE

GOODBYE, UKULELE

LEIGH NASH

Mansfield Press

Library and Archives Canada Cataloguing in Publication

Nash, Leigh, 1982-
    Goodbye, ukulele / Leigh Nash.

Poems.
ISBN 978-1-894469-50-0

    I. Title.

PS8627.A7755G66 2010   C811'.6   C2010-905914-X

Editor for the Press: Stuart Ross
Design: Denis De Klerck
Typesetting: Stuart Ross
Cover Photo: iStockphoto
Author Photo: Diane D'Amato

ONTARIO ARTS COUNCIL   Canada Council   Conseil des Arts
CONSEIL DES ARTS DE L'ONTARIO for the Arts   du Canada

The publication of *Goodbye, Ukulele* has been generously supported by
the Canada Council for the Arts and the Ontario Arts Council.

Mansfield Press Inc.
25 Mansfield Avenue, Toronto, Ontario, Canada M6J 2A9
Publisher: Denis De Klerck
www.mansfieldpress.net

For my mother

CONTENTS

EYE ON THE PRIZE

Hello, Mr. Magpie, how and where
is your wife? Time is peeling away
like a roll of sequins. There are ways
to keep you talking—mirrors, cameras, strings
of pearls, polished spoons—but you refuse
to answer, mouth a cast-iron vault. And then
there's the birthdate, the address,
the correctly spelled name, lined up
on the windowsill, just out of reach. It's lonely,
this one-two step with both hands
in your pockets, shadow
puppets without the light. Who
will hug a scavenger? Somewhere,
a silent alarm rings in an empty room
and no one pulls the trigger. Don't let the door
hit you on the way out.

The teller wraps shiny hair around
an index finger, thinks, Oh my god,
what are you talking about here.

A SUIT OF LIGHT

That was some morning: clouds scattered
like wisdom teeth in a silvery bowl, the sky
a honeydew with a spoonful missing. You
sucking on a lemon with one hand
on your hip. *I wish you were here* scrawled
in the tub's grime, the curtain
a sleepy eyelid. Something I wish

I'd never pulled back. Hanging
in the closet, a yawning moth hole: I
watched you shuffle across a blank stage
and disappear off-screen. A delicate bomb
ticked down like a mallet apologizing
to the sweet side of a bass drum. Turquoise
seeped in at the edges. A lengthening. A longing.

GONE FISHING

I've talked to my eye-
care specialist and he assures me the stars
are not asterisks to my thoughts.

How does he stay so organized? I have to stop
myself from lunging at mirrors and wheel
spokes, windows—

I wonder what they taste like. Oysters
come to mind, dense as cold spoons. Or lemons.

The kitchen sink is full of dishwater and it's starting
to rise. One of these days I'll lose an arm.
A fingernail. I'll be a real catch.

A SPOTLIGHT ILLUMINATES THE LIGHT SWITCH

Is there a hole in my eyelid?

Is it a June bug?

A molehill?

Can you hear the disrepair?

Can you read me the news?

Can you read it like a lullaby?

Can you whisper when the crowd grows quiet?

Can you whisper when they call my name?

Can I make a phone call?

Do you have a quarter?

How about now?

What if I miss the parade?

What if I mispronounce apropos?

Why won't you answer the phone?

Is that a hole in your chest?

Is it the size of my thumb?

Will you lay with me awhile?

Is it dark where you are?

BLACKOUT

July dips into white flowers,
charcoal grills, traffic jams. The power's

out. Flashlights kettle
the ceiling. Cooling end to end, candles gasp
at the muffled weather.

Filaments exhale.
Peeling kitchen wallpaper swoons

over full freezers stinking
of dark, burnt sighs.

IT'S PARIS IN THE TWENTIES

*"Fairy tales do not tell children the dragons exist. Children
already know that dragons exist. Fairy tales tell children the
dragons can be killed."*
—G. K. Chesterton

The gas dial hovers above red, refusing
to dip. It's been broken for a week
but the tank hasn't run dry. Is this
what I've been praying for all these years?

Above the treeline, the weather roils
like a burning lake; I look for its reflection
in the sweaty curve of your ear.

The passenger seat belt hangs like a snapped noose.

A sad ballet of parade floats
trails my Cadillac: a sinking armada
of tattered streamers. One red balloon
clings to a wooden cross.

Blue sky obstructs everything.
Blue sky and those wispy white clouds,
an obvious background.

MURMUR

Whales are suffering from seasonal
affective disorder, beaching themselves
by the truckload, starved for light.

They say vitamin D is essential
for a healthy heart. They say a whale's
heart is as big as a car. Yesterday I rode

the bus to the waterfront, climbed
into the lake face first. Both halves
of my brain melted into an oily sleep.

When I woke I was typing a telegram:
send defibrillator stop hearts
everywhere are giving up

IDEALLY, YOU DON'T WANT TO PLAGIARIZE ANYONE

Into this golden silence we lowered our spoons
like stray thoughts of a lost planet.
Every other house has someone living in it;
I was the one with the cool glass of water.
We would all wear handsomely tailored life jackets,
attracting bees like honey,
with absolutely zero effect.
It is morning, isn't it morning, it's morning.

There was sugar all over the table,
and words cruised paths through forests
to the crown of my skull.
Our mule took big, lonesome steps in her stall.
A full-blooded moon was foaming in our faces.

LET'S TAKE A CUE FROM THE CATHOLICS

The Virgin Mary appeared
in my bathtub this morning, legs
pressed together into one scaly fin
the colour of your eyes. I climbed
in and held her as she scrubbed
my face clean, songs slipping
from beneath her tongue.

She was too delicate to survive,
so I dried her out, set her on the shelf
with my collection of splinters,
olive pits, the things I fear.

I've been collecting for a while
now, and I'm no closer to figuring out
right from wrong—but it sure is nice
to have pinned down so much beauty.

MEANINGFUL LOVE

after John Ashbery

Yesterday was filled with wet boots,
crumpled newspapers in the gutters,
each page bearing your name in bold.
For the first time, it felt like fall—
sound the trumpets. The ocean's
swelling like a clogged bathtub, and
I got rid of the book of fairy tales.

The horizon is the horizon is an edgy profile
in a steamy bathroom mirror. Yesterday,
your breath left a hot "O" on my
windshield. I manoeuvred down Yonge Street
with one eye on the porthole, then
pawned my old car, bought a ticket to the funhouse

and kept on driving the point home.
Streamers the colour of your skin
hung from the rafters, fluttering
in the heat of imagination. What
could happen next. What won't. I
found myself back here at six o'clock,

whining into the telephone about discounted
knives that slice through tin
cans, pineapples, hardened
hearts flapping like swallows
with clipped wings; is there a guarantee,
is it worth time spent
pondering possible "side effects."

VENUS

Together, we are
a constellation, this bed
our night sky.

Pitted moons locked in
orbital conversation,
we excavate belly,
breast beneath milky
blankets—

ignore morning,
its copper
trap.

THE KIDS WERE AT SUNDAY SCHOOL

Fifteen miles from grace
a turtledove flew into their windshield.

He didn't say a word, started
the wipers—

and grey matter charged
the window, hid itself
in her hair.

A REAL THORN IN MY SIDE

I wolfed down three hearts.
They were salty as olives,
delicious. This was supposed to be
conducive to great work. Instead,
the gas bill arrived twice this
week, and the cat ate my chequebook
and vomited incorrect addition
on the rug. I'm tired of cleaning up
someone else's mess. What
would it take to come home
to windows glowing
like gift boxes, a smoky fire,
a dinner party where all the guests
wore fancy hats and screamed,
where I didn't have to lift a finger.

LOVE LETTER

Out there, there's a pigeon
plopped on the TV antenna
like a dollop of mouldy sour cream.
The light's pointing the wrong way—
your shirt's got one too many
buttons undone and I'm tired

of pinch-hitting. I've taken
your jar of pennies, its smell
of skinned knees. A refrigerator,
door ajar, the discovery
of an egg carton, eggs with yolks
sucked clean out through pinholes.

Is it raining yet, there?

STRANGE ATTRACTORS

"Edward Lorenz, the father of Chaos Theory, dies in Cambridge.
Somewhere, a butterfly twitches."
—Toronto Star, *May 4, 2008*

Tweezers, glittering pins seed
in plastic cups. You, relaxed
for easy mounting, hung out to dry.

Initial conditions looked good: an excess
of moths erupted from the chimney
and we pinched the flames out with our fingertips.

I'm told the killing jar leaves less chance
of damage, that it's easier to control
the outcome—then, an errant wing flap. Silver
thick with years of tarnish. A bloody
heart with one bite missing.

Our house has a puddle for a front lawn, said Tess.
Jump in it, said James Reddy. He picked egg out of his teeth
                                        with a fingernail.
NO! she screamed. I'm not jumping in that dirty river.
The cicadas stretched their legs.
Tess rubbed her hands together, *whishwhishwhish.*
Shhhhh, said James Reddy. I'm listening.
They listened together to a cavalry of bees, or toasters,
                                        or lawnmowers.
They sat side-by-each on the porch's step.
They wiggled their toes.
A foot over, the river began to grow.
Small waves licked the grass.
The breeze picked up.
Tess tugged her short brown pigtails.
James Reddy said, Can't you sit still?
No, she replied, I'm trying to make my hair grow.
On the horizon: a motorboat.

A flash and the sun disappeared, a stamped-out cigarette.
Then the boot heel lifted and the clouds winked.

The air around the porch wavered.
The river soaked the grass through.
That was a good trick, Tess agreed.
The sun cracked under its own weight.

You wear water, a mantle pulled tight. Lie low, provide contrast to the plateaux, good grazing. A smooth forehead in stern relief / Bony shoulders in a crowd. Change renders aloof sidewalks alluvial. A depression lurks, low hanging and widespread / Shorelines funnel out of reach, sheets lost in the night. Runoff fractures the basin / A scab: rusty earth a thumbprint thigh-high and swelling. Bodies buried under seams. Unassuming and overgrown / Ribbons in the wind. A sheer face, jagged hug of hanging valley. Scoured out by glaciers, a cool spray of Queen Anne's lace tossed roughly to the floor / A cavity, the tooth black and then an empty socket. A lockjawed long nap. Aged peat smokes the palate; preserves weather, weight, builds coal. Lathers, repeats / Dustbowled. Topsoil slips through the wind's fingers, a heavily plucked bass string. Silk dressing gowns, silt-dashed lashes, settling at last / A pitched tent, A-framed. Outside: rain. Tributaries run the walls like a bird's serrated footprints. The unzipped door an open mouth / Lunar cloister, the inside of a silkworm's cocoon. Along the shore, wind licks the skeletal hulls. Ghosts finger the frost / A fishbone caught at the back of the throat. No one could have predicted the small scales, the translucence—the slight slip flickering in rearview.

ATLAS

Cut out my shoulder
blades, flash-freeze
them at −83 degrees.

Maybe
when they thaw
they'll be softer, better
able to carry
our weight.

SWIMMER'S EAR

Three down: laps speak in the exotic
drone of helicopters, old refrigerators
and warm beer. Today, I listen
for the knife sharpener's bell from the back
yard—hold my breath until the truck passes,
then lick the lawnmower's rusty
blades clean, my arms flailing like a waxwing's
wings. I'm the pedestrian wandering
the bottom of the seashell, waiting
to be put up to someone's ear.
Can you hear me?

DAY TRIP

This day beetles forward
careening red eyelid on
a two-lane Yucatán road
110 km/h

Glass eyeballs unblink
chew up scenery, plow
past the tinted windows
of tourist vans

The most earth with no
earth, almond trees burst
from lime rock, low bushes
bear pink

Avocados; dogs spill sideways
in the sun, feral
ribs thin inlets

Corrugated towns chatter

Rusty graveyards swallow
pastel crosses row, row
crumbling plaster tombs
thousand-year-old stone
overgrown with lilies, bougainvillea

Waist-high girls and boys embrace
the shade of ledges
the missing teeth
of doorways, gutted windows

INTO THE WOOD CHIPPER

The maple throws up its arms
in fright. Oh, it says with each
hack. Oh.

All the keys tossed
out over the years, potential
heirs—

weeded out. The struggle, lately,
to stop the balding.

The wind in the upper branches hums
Oh, la dee da.

RESPONSE TO DEATH

Hello Headquarters?
           Hello, Headquarters?

LET'S READ IT TOMORROW

Jesus this, Jesus that: it's becoming
a refrigerator's hum. The lines

on my bifocals keep shifting,
skipping a's and j's and g's
across the page like flat stones.

Upstairs, a phone rings behind
a locked door. I can't remember
whose room it is,

but last week a flaming
heart appeared in the wood and none
of the keys fit the lock

anymore. Unread newspapers
are piling up on the kitchen table

and the answering machine—well,
I keep hoping that if I don't answer,

maybe they'll double
the offer.

WHEN YOU HAVE TO

An invisible letter
taped to the turquoise fridge:

it's for you, the corners crimped
from the leaking roof.

Y's fly close to the rafters
like too-white seagulls.
Their messages are invisible, too.

Out in the street they don't know
what to do with us, us sitting here
gnawing on the alphabet.

A QUESTION REGARDING BATS

From what direction do bats leave a cave? Which way do bats always turn when exiting a cave? Why do bats turn when leaving a cave? Do bats exit a cave to the left? Do bats always turn left when leaving a cave? Do bats always turn right when exiting a cave? Which way do bats turn when flying out of a cave? Bats, when leaving a cave, will always go in what direction? A bat will always turn in which direction when leaving a cave? Why does the mammal bat always turn left when flying out of a cave? Why can't bats turn right?

GRANULE

Sugar, here
slight beneath shaken hand
cut quick to bone.

Blanched by sun, crow
bodies lie, hot air
pooling in empty ribs.

Misinterpreted heads
roll.

MIDNIGHT—7:30 A.M., VARADERO

I did it all for the scent of your sunscreen;
the light crawling under the door.
The deep, even keel of sleep.

Twenty kilometres of white sand
unrolls like a starched sleeve.
The view pauses, the inhale
before your answer.

TIME SHARE

Wool sweats, a haze
on the horizon. Ten degrees: gloves,

hats, red wine. Out on the lake
two loons bob, corks

in a half-empty bottle. Light
bellows. Piled fly carcasses insulate

window sills. A fireplace
ignites with the flick

of a switch.

WRECKED

Ribs slick the sand
chipped out by blue plastic shovels,
      a first holiday
in the shadow of the Southampton Harbour Light.

Unburied, rotting hull arches
over bleached shore, a worm-
eaten rainbow
        leaning against the grey sky.

Meticulous photos
catalogue the gash
in her side

and only the locals know
where she was reburied.

Bright
bulldozers push
the burnt summer sun.

TWILIGHT IN BELLEVUE SQUARE PARK

You, crooked.
Ground from old
photo booths, cheap
hotels. Sepia eyes fade
into this landscape, parked
bikes limber against chain-link.
The sky purple, your lips open.

FOR SALE

A lemonade stand   abandoned

cardboard sign, crude
red letters capsize

empty, sticky pitchers

puckered lemon halves
gut the sidewalk

forgotten coins in a pile
of sugar

INTRODUCTION TO DECAPITATING A KISS

If the aim is true, a kiss
is one of the most intimate
and painless forms of experience.

There's no right instrument. If blunt
or the executioner clumsy, multiple
strokes may be required to sever
a kiss. When you're ready, it is wise
to give a new partner a coin
so he does his job with care.

Not getting your proper money's worth?
You've come to the right place.

HOW TO SCALP A NAP

The standard technique
for scalping: place a knee
between the shoulders. It will not
interfere with your sleep. Cut a long arc
in the front, taking your schedule
into consideration. Pull back on the hair.

Your midafternoon nap
survived, facial features may droop.
Dozing right will make a tight braid.

GUTTING, A BATH

Get the cleanest kill possible, head
or soft mess. The bathroom smells
of second choice. Bleed the carcass
on the other side of the door; slope
with head facing downhill. The dog
kicks his legs before, during and
after. Hair fanning out like musk:
be careful not to scalp. Avoid inhaling.
Don't come into contact
with the meat.

THINGS FALL APART

The last day of swim unit. Brandy hit
the water first, a hot knife. The thing
with diving is that you don't dive:
you believe in your own physics.

The thing with girls like Brandy is they peak
too early. Sure, she looks good, her boobs
busting out of a one-piece, but like Dad says,
that'll go. Over my shoulder, instead of water,

a giant nest of doughy nipples shimmers
and I can already hear my vertebrae
snapping in anticipation.

FLICK

A lob catches the updraft—
another swing, another
fosh in the mitt. Another burned-
out switch. Another afternoon
running in a short-
circuited circle, both feet
in the bucket. Today,
the sky's the litmus.
Buck up. Tell your pinch
hitter to keep his eye
on the wheel,
                    his hands
on the ace.

DECEMBER

The tree's needles ride my sock heels
to the living room's wool rug: moon-
shine plantations spring up between
the whorls. The whole thing reeks
of piracy and white
lightning, but every morning
before going to bed, the little
men in felted hats screech
Hello, ask How are you
feeling today, as I slosh
through their flame tests
on my way to the bathroom.

GOODBYE, UKULELE

They're unrolling the red carpet, one
dusty footprint at a time. In the corner,
a silver-haired couple sways in a lazy
loop through a puddle of champagne.

The shadows stink of blackcurrant, of matches
burned down to toothpicks. I watch the whisper
of mustard on my tie dissipate.

I can't remember the first words I said to you.

Oysters climb back into their shells,
pretending no one's home. In crystal bowls,
ice hardens into cubes; butter into pats.
The trout's glassy eye records everything.

I remember when I was a twinkle in my own eye.

The speaker goes on about hair loss, Sundays,
and how the earth will never stop shifting
beneath our feet. A smattering of applause
reminds me I've forgotten my umbrella.

Confetti drops from the rafters, a shiny haze
of plastic O's. I'm scared to look up, even though

I've never been afraid of heights.
Goodbye, ukulele,
goodbye.

ICU

Little shipwrecks
bump against the hulls of other
wrecks, waiting to see whose lifeboat
will be the first to sink.

LINEAR A

Syllables slotted into weather-beaten tetherballs, hull-less ships
docking in the dark.

TUMOUR

There is a grace
in shaking hands, skin
cupping brittle
bone, rough
red, vital. Hands
that used to breed
bees. Silken
honey tender
under the tongue.

Sift through the papery grey ash
      white fractals of bone.

See how those hives
      are dust.

LINEAR B

Hands cradle a common suffix; frozen deer drown in metre.

A HUNDRED LIES

This one was red, a rose, a rosary: I blinked my way
through the highway's long line of cars, bowed
in deference to the tail lights. It is a fact that catastrophes
mean nothing to most people. I hear

there's a book of answers, probably
tucked at the back of the tallest shelf, where no
one would think to look. Beads of sweat shiver
along the window's hairline. Can I come over

if I promise to swallow six knives, one right after
the other—though they all must be the same
size. I imagine the shiny blades
as hoisted sails in my stomach, keeling into
acid as clear and colourless as water.
This makes me walk straight. When I cry,

my tears are pearls. They sprout wings,
flit away to softer clouds. Even my head
on the pillow isn't enough to pin them down. Me,

your lonely oyster, tucked in the back of the refrigerator
behind jars of strawberry jam, a tub of low-fat
margarine and curdling chowder. My insides
wring themselves like grieving hands. They say oysters
feel no pain, are suitable for vegan diets. I'm skeptical;
I've heard trees screaming over broken limbs.

Here is a list: a broken heart, an empty living
room, a white screen. Sometimes, a record player.

Yes, I listened to every word you ever said; I copied
them all down on scraps of loose-leaf. Whole sentences
have piled up and it'll be some party
when you finally break down that door. We have fewer

than ten words left to say to each other and none
of them is "I'm sorry" or "I love you" or "It's your turn
to clean out the fridge." Your voice
is radio static. Last night

I dreamt of licking the bottoms of burnt-out
shoes. This is the most sensual act I've undertaken
in years. I'm afraid to go out. Through a knothole
I watch snow fleck the sidewalk's edge, spittle
against cold lips. Why can't I keep my mouth shut.

A gathering storm marches down Main Street,
bearing white flags. Boot heels clatter and I stomp
in time. There's safety in numbers. There's safety
in finding the best place to hide. Remember, you held me—
in return, I drove along back roads, rolling
the dice. A wrong turn turned

out to be a blessing: I'm better

on even years. On subbing in an item from Column B
the ground shook. The house straightened out
and all the pictures huddled in the corners
of their frames, whispering about the end.

I wander from room to room
wearing nothing but breath, praying for more
accurate weather reports, convinced

that proof lies in the hypotenuse of icicles. Listless
as tinsel, you rove from one town to the next, sneezing
out blessings and broken promises. You earn

praise. Maybe even love. The good old days
continue to recede, ashamed of their failures.

Somewhere, a swan runs down a freeway, too shy
to take flight, having forgotten its awkward lightness.
Scientists sleep this off.

I'm determined to catch the fly buzzing around the ceiling
lamp. Then the horizon careens into view,
old friend, and settles in with a sigh.

REINCARNATION

At 9 a.m., buried
behind a grey veil,
the hills are still
green with spring
and the ferns shake
off the winter cold
as they unravel,
stretching long arms
towards the light.

I THOUGHT YOU WERE GIVING UP

Life's wagging and you sit there
lobbing butter knives. The good silver
heaped on the floor.

I've graphed it three times, written it out
longhand in binary. The numbers add up:

you're out in the cold and no one
is answering the door. Tomorrow,

the pumpkin goes out the window.

SIREN

Tucked inside happy hour,
old women are superstitious
and do not forget. We point
brooms at reeling gulls, swallow
the clock's cold, clicking tongue.

ON THE SIDE OF THE ROAD IN TURKEY

They give her
a necklace, made in—

Further on

smoking
                cigarettes?

Pale arms, sunlight

Men trade
                bargain, pockets
                        wait—

Beautiful, they say

                wave lilies

She leaves before
        one smoke between
                trains

on the platform
whistles

        unrest

after thirty years

She fingers the cheap
plastic beads   a stain
                her throat

Redder than raw muscle, an unearthed sunset,
fourth in line with an iron fist.
A worn-out welcome. Water—the largest
flash-in-the-pan, a giant slump, dried inlets
bright before the naked eye. Who's to interpret
the lava plains, the crater's aureoles? History
flirts with false promises, the existence
of mistakes on another planet.

Floods of carbon dioxide and rust
look good on paper—a waxy simulacra
or a collapsed vein. Rainmakers
wave their hands and landscapers fill in the gaps.
They're told, Don't fuck up. They're told
nothing is ever enough.

GRAVEYARD SHIFT

Black and white film, night
spooled on mute—a lock
picked clean. Admire

the kitchen's comfortable
clutter. The shovel's proper place
in the shed. A word so

insignificant that you would die
to hear it, just once more.

ALLOTMENT

It's a sign of the times: even double-
paned windows can't keep out

the moans of other people's errands.
So much motion is exhausting.

I tie my shoelaces loosely so they'll come
undone, give me an excuse to pause, but

lately, every sentence has been ending
with an exclamation point. The last book

I read burst into flames when I hit
the third chapter. I buried the ashes

in the backyard, sifting through layers
of grass, dead leaves, feathers. It's lonely

being alone. A bed of ferns blankets
the newly turned earth, softening

the blow, and every night this week
the sunset's been the colour

of raw hamburger, the clouds as final
as periods. I grow queasy reaching

for the top shelf, fingering the negative
spaces: I can never see what's up there,

just what it is I've touched.

I WASN'T SUGGESTING THAT YOU COULDN'T

John's heart, the size of a thumbtack, skips every other beat.
A room full of seagulls peck at each other's eyes.
Glitter flies off the ceiling fan on Tuesday afternoons.
Sarah's mouth opens, then closes, then opens.
Moths whisper sweet nothings to Alex's sweaters.
Jennifer's bicycle pedals off into the sunset.
The wheels yawn like open mouths.
A family of beavers moves in next door.
The house collapses a week later.
John plays pickup sticks and learns to knit.
Wings tickle the backs of Mark's eyelids.
They say the headaches will stop soon.
Sometimes Alice finds herself glaring at the horizon.
The dentist props open Alice's mouth.
When Todd closes his mouth, teeth litter his tongue like confetti.
The fridge is stocked with woolly socks.
The beer store has been out of beer for weeks.
Steve is antsy.
Steve picks at a scab on his knee until the valve breaks.
Water is everywhere.
Steve can't swim.
The beer store is fresh out of lifeboats.
The beavers are fresh out of sticks.
The water is a glittery mouth full of gold teeth.
The water is thirsty.

COMMUTE

And the afternoon puts on a brave face,
puts up a collar against the cold. Two days ago,
the weather vane found a new direction—
it hasn't moved since. There's smoke,
and then there's smoke.

On the street corner, a woman's wide mouth
is a church organ. Pedestrians scatter: one by one
they slip through the sidewalk grates. I'm left with a fistful

of weeds, a stomach full of ideas small as buttons.
The tailor tells me they'll never hold, but I'm
optimistic.

YOU SHOULD SEE THE GOLD STATUE OF ME
IN TRAFALGAR SQUARE

This season has turned into one of clouds
and more clouds. The road map leads from A
to B, then skips a few stops, and we end up
at the edge of that river; I can never
remember its name. The sun slants through trees
like butter knives, parsing the horizon
into manageable slices. I nurse

a longing for something better
than what's right now, the trundling up
of a neatly wrapped package, your name
hand-lettered in perfect script. Knowing
which string to tug first. Days puddle

around our ankles and we wade through. I like
to think there's more than choosing
appropriate footwear, that when the camera's
flash freezes our profile, someone will know what to do
with the photo: find the right frame, or burn the negative.

NOTES & ACKNOWLEDGEMENTS

"Ideally, You Don't Want to Plagiarize Anyone" is a cento derived from Dara Wier's *Selected Poems* (Wave Books, 2009) • "Meaningful Love" is a glosa on a poem of the same title by John Ashbery; the original can be found in *Where Shall I Wander: New Poems* (HarperCollins, 2005) • The lines in "A Response to Death" come from Tom Paxton's "Talking Vietnam Potluck Blues" • The questions in "A Question Regarding Bats" are derived from wiki. answers.com • Linear A is one of two linear and possibly syllabic scripts used in ancient Crete, and Linear B is the oldest surviving record of the Greek Mycenaean dialect. Both scripts share some of the same symbols, but using syllables associated with Linear B in Linear A writing produces words unrelated to any known language.

Earlier versions of some of these poems have appeared in *Existere, Carousel Magazine, Ottawa Arts Review, HARDSCRABBLE* and *The Puritan*; thanks to the respective editors • "Landforms" appeared as a chapbook of the same title from Apt. 9 Press (2010); many thanks to the delightful Cameron Anstee.

Heartfelt thank-yous to my family and friends; to Priscila Uppal and Chris Doda; to Ken Babstock and Dionne Brand; to the Roving Poetry Death Squad, and in particular Elisabeth de Mariaffi; to my talented editor (and friend), Stuart Ross, and Mansfield publisher Denis De Klerck. Thanks times a billion to Andrew Faulkner for your laughter and insight—you make every day brilliant.

 Leigh Nash is a Toronto-based writer, editor, and administrator. A graduate of the University of Guelph's MFA in Creative Writing program, she is a partner in the editing firm Re:word Communications, a co-founder of The Emergency Response Unit, and an executive member of the Scream Literary Festival. Her work has appeared in various print and online literary journals.